Society American Colonization

Exposition of the errors of the New York State Colonization Society in its late attacks on the American Colonization Society

Society American Colonization

Exposition of the errors of the New York State Colonization Society in its late attacks on the American Colonization Society

ISBN/EAN: 9783337153809

Printed in Europe, USA, Canada, Australia, Japan

Cover: Foto ©ninafisch / pixelio.de

More available books at **www.hansebooks.com**

OF THE ERRORS OF THE

New York State Colonization Society,

IN ITS LATE ATTACKS

ON THE

American Colonization Society.

NEW YORK :

MACDONALD & PALMER, PRINTERS, 733 BROADWAY

1870.

EXPOSITION

OF THE ERRORS OF THE

, NEW YORK STATE COLONIZATION SOCIETY,

IN ITS

LATE ATTACKS ON THE AMERICAN COLONIZATION SOCIETY.

A PAMPHLET of twenty-nine pages, entitled, "Statement of the New York State Colonization Society as to its Differences with the American Colonization Society," was published in March, 1870. It was soon followed by another, of fourteen pages, entitled, "Synopsis of the Effort made in behalf of the American Colonization Society, to get control of the field of the New York State Colonization Society, in violation of the pledge of non-interference."* These were preceded by a series of publications from the office of the

---

* These pamphlets are without signature, but the "Statement" was accompanied by the following, on a loose slip of colored paper :

"COLONIZATION OFFICE, ROOM 22, BIBLE HOUSE, }
"*New York, March* 15, 1870. }

"At the regular monthly meeting of the Board of Control of the New York State Colonization Society, held this day, the President of the Society, Hon. James W. Beckman, in the chair, a statement prepared by a Committee previously appointed, was reported complete, whereupon the Board passed the following resolution :

"*Resolved,* That the statement of this Society, as to its differences with the American Colonization Society, prepared and now presented to the Board of Control, be adopted, and copies be given to persons interested in the cause of African Colonization, whose minds may have been abused by the false statements put forth against this Society.

"A true copy from the minutes of the Board.

"J. M. GOLDBERG, *Recording Secretary.*"

The Society, therefore, is responsible for it. But it ought to be known that its President, by whose name it seems to be authenticated, and two other members of the Board, voted against its adoption.

State Society, beginning about June, 1869, arguing that funds should not be given to the American Colonization Society for sending out emigrants, because they were not needed ; nor for the promotion of education, because that Society could not lawfully receive or use them ; but should be given to the State Society, which had more comprehensive powers. These publications contain representations concerning matters of fact, which it appears to be a duty to correct.

THE "DIFFERENCES" IN NEW YORK.

The title-page of the "Statement" sophistically hides a very important fact. The "Differences" of the State Society were primarily and mainly with a very large and respectable portion of its own members. They had been growing for many years, and culminated, in New York, in November, 1869, when a new Society was formed, called the "New York Colonization Society." It was organized at a meeting called with the "cordial approval," in writing, of Samuel F. B. Morse, Moses Allen, Thomas De Witt, H. K. Corning, John N. McLeod, Wm. C. Alexander (N. J.), Talbot W. Chambers, Ambrose K. Ely, Hiram Ketchum, H. K. Bull, R. M. Olyphant, S. D. Alexander, Benjamin I. Haight, Joseph Holdich, J. McElroy, William H. Hallock, James C. Holden, S. Irenæus Prime, Henry Young, Burr Wakeman, John P. Crosby, T. C. M. Paton, Guy Richards, David M. Stone, Zachary Eddy, Theodore L. Mason, Joseph Kimball, A. S. Barnes, Francis B. Wheeler, S. M. Buckingham, C. J. Buckingham, Edward L. Beadle, Charles S. Hageman, Erastus Corning, Thomas W. Olcott, E. P. Prentice, A. E. Campbell, W. G. T. Shedd, John A. Stewart, T. H. Skinner, William Ives Budington, William Adams, John Hall, Henry Day, James Brown, C. H. McCormick, Jonathan Sturges, David Terry, L. H. King, George N. Titus, Henry C. Potter, William Dennistoun, Stewart Brown, J. Stanford Holme, George W. Jewett, Joseph W. Harper, Thomas D. Anderson, Robert Carter, H. B. Ridgaway, Caleb T. Rowe, S. D. Burchard, T. Ralston Smith, John Van Orden, J. D. Vermilye, Samuel Cooke, Henry Rose, William F. Morgan, John Hancock, R. S. Storrs, Jr., N. H. Schenck, William Walker, Norman Seaver, Henry G. Marquand, H. D. Ganse, Thomas Jeremiah.

Of these, Dr. De Witt was President, Messrs. Allen, Ketchum, and Haight were Vice-Presidents, and some others were officers of the New York State Society. The officers of the new Society were as follows, viz.:

PRESIDENT.

Prof. Samuel F. B. Morse, LL. D. - - - - - - New York.

VICE-PRESIDENTS.

Hon. Erastus Corning - - - - - - - - Albany.
Rt. Rev. Horatio Potter, D. D. - - - - - New York.
Rev. John N. McLeod, D. D. - - - - - - "
Stephen M. Buckingham, Esq. - - - - - - Poughkeepsie.
Rev. Samuel W. Fisher, D. D. - - - - - Utica.
Rev. Walter Clark, D. D. - - - - - - Buffalo.

SECRETARY AND TREASURER.

Almon Merwin, Esq. - - - - - - - - New York.

BOARD OF MANAGERS.

H. K. Corning, Esq., New York.	John P. Crosby, Esq., New York.
H. K. Bull, Esq., "	C. H. McCormick, Esq., "
Henry Day, Esq., "	Ambrose K. Ely, Esq., "
Rev. S. D. Alexander, D. D., "	Burr Wakeman, Esq., "
Rev. Wm. F. Morgan, D. D., "	Rev. David Terry, "
Rev. Benj. I. Haight, D. D., "	John Van Orden, Esq., "
Rev. H. C. Potter, D. D., "	Rev. Zachary Eddy, D. D., Brooklyn.
Rev. H. L. King, "	Rev. W. I. Budington, D. D., "
Rev J. S. Holme, D.D., "	Theodore L. Mason, M. D., "
James C. Holden, Esq., "	Wm. H. Hallock, Esq., "
T. C. M. Paton, Esq., "	Thomas W. Olcott, Esq., Albany.
J. D. Vermilye, Esq., "	E. P. Prentice, Esq., "

EXECUTIVE COMMITTEE.

Rev. Benj. I. Haight, D.D., New York.	H. K. Bull, Esq, New York.
Rev. S. D. Alexander, D. D., "	Jacob D. Vermilye, Esq., New York.
Henry G. Marquand, Esq., "	

The dissatisfaction which led to this result had been growing for many years; especially since the change of policy which followed the death of Anson G. Phelps, Jr., President of the Society, in May, 1858.

THE " DIFFERENCES " AT WASHINGTON.

At the annual meeting of the Directors of the American Colonization Society, on Tuesday, January 18, 1870, the Committee on Credentials were the same persons as in 1869, and its Chairman the same as in 1868 and 1867. Among the papers referred to them, was one showing a pecuniary basis for six Delegates, and six only, from the State of New York. Other papers showed the appointment of six Delegates by each of the two Societies existing in that State ; all the twelve claiming seats on the same pecuniary basis, which was sufficient only for six. Another paper was the following :

NEW YORK CITY, *December* 1, 1869.

We, the undersigned, do hereby certify, that we are not in sympathy with the policy and acts of the New York State Colonization Society, and that the donations which we have made during the year 1869, to the American Colonization Society, were not intended by us to increase the representation of the said New York State Colonization Society at the annual meeting of the American, or Parent Society. And we do further certify, that we are in sympathy with the New York Colonization Society, organized in the City of New York, November 25, 1869, and do hereby approve of such organization. And we desire that all our benefactions made during the year 1869, to the American Colonization Society, should, for the purpose of representation, be considered as made through the said New York Colonization Society.

Henry Young.	Edward L. Beadle.	Burr Wakeman.
H. K. Corning.	S. M. Buckingham.	Guy Richards.
A. C. Brown.	E. P. Prentice.	James M. Mills.
Samuel F. B. Morse.	Thomas W. Olcott.	Z. Stiles Ely.
Benj. I. Haight.	Thomas Jeremiah.	Geo. W. Jewett.
A. S. Barnes.	Moses Allen.	M. J. Myers.
H. K. Bull. ·	Stewart Brown.	Wm. C. Sterling.
John A. Stewart.	James Brown.	Erastus Corning.
S. Irenaeus Prime.	Wm. Dennistoun.	Theodore L. Mason.
Isaac H. Knox.	M. Few.	William H. Hallock.
Jas. C. Holden.	F. F. Chrystie.	Henry Day.
John P. Crosby.	M. F. Tillotson.	

The " Statement " does not assert, but obtrusively and repeatedly implies, that these gentlemen, and those on the two preceding lists, did not act from their own judgment in view of facts known to themselves, but were the dupes and tools of the Traveling Secretary, who was instigated by " another stipendiary " of the Parent Society. Formally to refute such an imputation on such men, would be treating it with more appearance of respect than either justice or decency permits.

The Committee was also informed, without contradiction, that the donations of the signers of that paper had been about $3,000, the sum necessary to constitute a basis for six Delegates, and that the other donors, so far as known, were in sympathy with the new Society. The New York State Society neither had nor claimed any pecuniary basis, even to the amount of a dollar, except these very same donations, save the sum of $32.75 disbursed by its Corresponding Secretary in Liberia. Their only argument was, that, under a certain resolution of the Board of Directors, passed in 1863, all moneys received from any persons in the State of New York must be credited to them, as a basis of representation. But that resolution was passed without any reference to a case like this, of two Societies in the same State, and the Directors were as competent to set it aside as they were to pass it. The Constitution made no provision for such a case. The money could not be made a basis of representation for the State Society, in direct opposition to the expressed will of the donors. There was no constitutional provision, or any law whatever, against the formation of a second Society in New York or in any other State. Those who formed the new Society had an unquestionable right to do so. They had made themselves auxiliary by their Constitution, and had contributed funds accordingly.

With these facts before them, the Committee made a report in part, which was adopted, giving seats to the Delegates from other States, concerning whose right there was no question. When the Board was thus constituted, they reported further, that the six Delegates from the New York Society were entitled to seats, and recommended that those sent as Delegates from the New York State Society be invited to sit as corresponding members.

One of the gentlemen last mentioned opposed the adoption of this report, in a speech, largely from manuscript, extending through the remaining business hours of that day and far into the next. After a brief reply by a Delegate from the New York Society, a Director moved that the subject be referred to a special Committee, who, he thought, would be able to report a compromise acceptable to all parties. After consultation with all parties, this Committee reported, recommending that certain sums which the

New York State Society was said to have expended for education in Liberia, should be recognized as a basis of representation for five of the Delegates appointed by that Society ; the sixth being entitled to a seat as a Director for life. They also reported a resolution, to take the place of that passed in 1863, providing for such cases in future years.

The Committee were unanimous in this report. No person, from New York or elsewhere, made any objection to it. It was understood by the Committee, and by the Board of Directors, that the Delegates from the New York State Society all accepted it as a final settlement of the controversy, and with that understanding, it was unanimously adopted by the Board.

But these hopes were destined to disappointment. On Thursday—not, as the arrangement of matters in the " Statement" seems to imply, on Tuesday, before the Committee on Credentials had made their final report,—but on Thursday afternoon, when the Directors were about to adjourn, a Delegate from the New York State Society rose and read a " memorial," *demanding* that the Directors should " withdraw all agencies from the State of New York, and leave its territory to be canvassed by the New York State Society's agents," and offered a resolution to the same effect. As the only "agency" of the Parent Society then in New York was that of the Traveling Secretary, then laboring there at the formal request of the New York Colonization Society, this movement was evidently aimed at him, and at that Society. It reopened the whole controversy, which had been understood to have been finally settled, and appeared to many of the Directors to be a plain breach of the faith pledged in that settlement. A motion was made, to lay the memorial and the resolution on the table. The presenter of the memorial demanded the yeas and nays. They were taken. The yeas were fifteen. Among them were two of the five Delegates from the New York State Society, one of whom was its President, by whose signature the memorial was authenticated. The memorial, the "Statement" informs us, had been prepared in New York, and his signature was doubtless then affixed to it. Now, he voted to lay it and the accompanying resolution on the table. The nays were, the presenter of the memorial, two other Delegates from the same Society, the Secretary of that Society, being a Life Director, and one Delegate from Pennsylvania; in all, five. Fourteen Directors had retired from the meeting, supposing that its business was finished. It is known that they would all have voted in the affirmative, making the total in favor of laying it on the table, twenty-nine.

Another motion was then made by the same Delegate from the State Society, that all papers and letters read before the Executive Committee on a certain occasion should be reported to the Board and copied into the records. As this could not be done without greatly prolonging the session, and could not be of any use for any purpose, except that of more conveniently continuing the controversy, this motion also was laid on the table. So ended the exhibition of these "differences," at that meeting. But a charge made during its progress may be most conveniently considered here.

THE CHARGE OF FALSEHOOD.

This charge against the Traveling Secretary was made in the long speech on Tuesday and Wednesday, and is repeated in the "Statement" as follows :

"There was also an allegation in one of these letters of the Traveling Secretary, that,

"The amount the Parent Society received in cash from the New York State Colonization Society since 1849, nearly twenty years, is less than $12,000, and the entire amount obtained has not averaged $1,000 a year for the last fifteen years," "which is simply untrue."

In proof of its untruth, the "Statement" gives the following table of such receipts, compiled from the *African Repository :*

1849. February and July	$6,000 00
1850. February, June, and July	7,300 00
1853. January and August	3,898 02
1854. May	33 00
1855. January and April	1,060 00
1856. February and September	2,907 67
1857. January, February, March, and April	3,105 76
1858. January	922 90
1862. January	786 39
1863. February	200 00
	$26,213 74

This proof of falsehood will not bear cross-examination. Let us look at it year by year.

1849.—The $6,000 received *in* 1849 was not received "*since* 1849*,*" and has nothing to do with the truth of the Secretary's "allegation."

1850.—The *Repository* for February acknowledges two sums, one of $3,000 and one of $1,000, as received "from the 20th of December, 1849, to the 20th of January, 1850." The $3,000 was received as a loan, October 17, 1849. A letter from Rev. J. B. Pinney, dated December 21, 1849, stated that it had been made a donation by vote of the Board of the State Society on the Monday evening last previous. It was received as a donation, therefore, *in* 1849, and not "since 1849," and must be deducted.

The *Repository* for June acknowledges the receipt of $1,800, being eighteen donations of one hundred dollars each, to the Parent Society, from persons there named. They were procured by Gerard Hallock, Esq., at the request of Rev. Wm. McLain, Financial Secretary. The money was handed to Rev. J. B. Pinney, May 10th, to be paid over to Mr. McLain, and was paid over the same day. It was never the property of the State Society, nor in its treasury, nor at its disposal. See the first article in that number of the *Repository.*

1853.—The $3,178.23, in January, was not cash then paid to the Parent Society, but the amount reported by the New York State Society as having been spent by itself in 1852, and allowed as a basis of representation.

1854, May.—The $33 was given by citizens of New York to the Parent Society.

1856, February.—The $407.67 was spent by the State Society and admitted as a basis of representation.

1857.—The $30 in February and $30 in April, from donors to the Parent Society for life memberships, and the $1,045.76 in March, being not cash, but an order on the Society's agent at Monrovia for goods, must be subtracted.

1858.—The $922.90, being $153.59 for goods at Monrovia, and $769.31 for "sundry expenses of emigrants paid by" the Treasurer of the State Society, must be deducted.

1862.—The $786.39, expended by the State Society "for the

passage and support of emigrants," and allowed as a basis of representation, must be deducted.

These sums, deducted from their total, $26,213.74, leave $8,979.79. To this add $70, March, 1860, and $66.34, February, 1861, overlooked by them, and we have $9,116.13, as the total amount actually paid in cash by the New York State Colonization Society to the Parent Society " since 1849," and acknowledged in the *African Repository*, to which they appeal ; being $2.883.87 " less than $12,000 ;" so that Dr. Orcutt's "allegation," instead of being " simply untrue," is strictly true.

This proof that they have falsely accused the Traveling Secretary of falsehood, and made a false exhibit of their own cash payments to the Parent Society, can neither be rebutted nor evaded. None of the sums deducted are said in the *Repository* to have been received " in cash," though some of them were so received, but not from them ; and of some, the contrary is expressly stated in the places to which they refer. For example, $1,045.76 in March, 1857 ; $922.90 in January, 1858 ; and $786.39 in January, 1862. That they know the difference, appears from their not claiming as a cash payment, $2,713.99,.acknowledged in similar form in January, 1860 ; an acknowledgment which they must have seen, for the sum is claimed in another table on the same page of their " Statement." Nor can they escape by saying that paying high prices for the passage of emigrants by trading vessels from New York, and turning over to the Parent Society surplus goods which they had improvidently sent to Monrovia, is the same as paying cash into the treasury of the Parent Society. It is not the same, nor even its equivalent in value.

It is a noticeable fact, that the whole amount which they claim as paid in cash since the death of A. G. Phelps, Jr., in May, 1858, was only $986.39, and the amount actually paid only, $336.34. Since his death, there had been a gradual change of policy in that Society, leading to dissatisfaction among its members, and ultimately to the formation of the new Society.

ASSUMPTIONS OF THE NEW YORK STATE SOCIETY.

The reasonings and appeals in all these publications of the State Society rest on certain assumptions, which can by no means be admitted. They are,

1. That the Constitution and Charter of the American Colonization Society restrain it from doing certain things which are indispensable to successful colonization in Africa.

2. That the Constitution and Charter of the New York State Colonization Society is more comprehensive, and authorize it to do those things, indispensable to successful colonization, which the Parent Society can not do ; especially, to promote education in Liberia.

3. That, by an ancient compact between the two Societies, still in force, the New York State Society has an exclusive right to solicit donations for colonization within the limits of the State of New York ; and that the Parent Society has no right, in any way, to ask aid from any person in that State, without first obtaining permission from the State Society.

4. That a time had come, in which it was the duty of that State Society to enforce its exclusive right, in order to procure funds with which to execute certain projects of its own, distinct from the work of the Parent Society.

A theory of that kind seems to have been working in the minds of some officers and members of that Society for some years, modifying its action and producing disaffection among its members, as has been stated; but it was never brought out distinctly, in print, till some time in 1869. The attempt to enforce it led the giving friends of the Parent Society to form a new Society, which should be, as they say, " in fact, as well as professedly, auxiliary to the American Colonization Society." These assumptions must be examined.

THE LEGAL POWERS OF THE TWO SOCIETIES.

The Constitution of the Parent Society declares its object to be, " to promote and execute a plan for colonizing," etc. This has always, and rightly, been understood to include the doing of all things necessary to colonizing successfully, though not specified ; such as procuring vessels for transportation, food for the temporary subsistence of colonists, and schools for their education. Its charter authorizes it to use its funds as it "shall determine to be most conducive to the colonizing, with their own consent, in Africa, of free people of color." The charter of the New York State Society, by the last clause of the second section, where its "business

and objects" are specified, limits it to "measures conducive to
the objects of African colonization." The coincidence in language
is remarkable. The Constitution of the New York State Society
claims nothing which the Parent Society may not do, and nothing
which it has not been doing, except in the last clause of its second
article : "and also generally to improve the condition of the colored population of our country." This, however, its charter does not
authorize it to do ; and in doing it, it would not act as a Colonization Society at all. In no matter "conducive" to successful
colonization, are the corporate powers of the New York State
Society any more ample than those of the American.

They claim, indeed, that the enemies of the Parent Society accused
it of a very narrow policy, and that they, instead of repelling the
slander, as they ought to have done, admitted it, and made their
own policy broader, to conciliate the accusers. If this were true,
it would show that they made concessions unjust and injurious to
the Parent Society at the outset, and have been on a platform of
semi-hostility ever since. The fact seems to be, that they met
those slanders by specifying, in their Constitution, some of the de-
tails which were only implied in that of the Parent Society.

THE RIGHT TO PROMOTE EDUCATION.

It is on the Parent Society's want of power to promote education, that these circulars and pamphlets chiefly insist. The discovery of this deficiency is quite recent. The Parent Society
claimed that power and avowed that purpose as early as January,
1817, and has been exercising it, as occasions have been presented,
ever since 1826. (See its Annual Report for 1870, pages 14 to 21,
where its habitual action, continuing to the present time, is shown
by reference to documents.) This deficiency was unknown to
Anson G. Phelps, Sen., long President of the New York State Society, who, as one of the Auditing Committee of the Parent Society,
every year from 1839 to his death in 1853, sanctioned many bills
for expenditures in promoting education. It was unknown to the
Rev. J. B. Pinney, when, as Governor of Liberia, he expended the
Society's money in establishing and supporting schools. It was
unknown to him even in January, 1869, when he earnestly urged
the Directors of the Parent Society to energy and liberality in

promoting education; and was then unknown to William Tracy, Esq., Delegate from the New York State Society, who so ably supported the views of Dr. Pinney. It was unknown to the Executive Committee of the Parent Society, when, April 2, 1869, they passed a resolution instructing their agents to collect funds for education in Liberia, and when their appeal for such funds was published in the *Repository* for May. There is no evidence that it was known to any officer or member of the State Society previously to the meeting of its Board, May 28, 1869. At that meeting a resolution was adopted, that the Society would, for the present, "direct its efforts chiefly to aid the people of Liberia in the establishment and maintenance of schools," and some other improvements. Soon after, some time in June, a circular of eight pages was issued, announcing that determination of the Society, and quoting a passage from its charter, showing that it was authorized to provide and expend funds for that purpose, and a passage from the Constitution of the Parent Society, implying, by the way in which it was quoted, that that Society had other business more appropriate. But this somewhat gentle and indefinite insinuation was not fully interpreted till September 1, 1869, when a printed letter to the Rev. Dr. Durbin, from "a member of both the American and New York State Colonization Society," was issued from the office of the New York State Colonization Society, in which its author asserted, and endeavored to prove, that "if the American Colonization Society collects funds and pays them over for the purposes of education, it is violating its Constitution and charter." The discovery was certainly most opportune, being made when the Traveling Secretary of the American Society was collecting funds in New York and the neighboring States, both for emigration and education, with such success, that there was danger,—to use the language of the "Synopsis,"—"of all collections being made by Dr. Orcutt and sent to the American Society, leaving nothing for the New York State Society to even pay its clerk hire or office rent." In the presence of such a danger, such a discovery was distressingly needed, to change the course of the current of donations. Who believes it, besides the inventors, remains to be ascertained.

THE ALLEGED COMPACT.

They allege a " Compact," that the New York State Society should occupy its own territory exclusively.

Such a "compact," or "pledge of non-interference," is repeatedly alleged in the "Statement" and "Synopsis;" and under it they claim the right to exclude the Parent Society from asking aid in the work of Colonization, directly or indirectly, from any person in the State of New York ; and they claim not only the exclusive right to collect funds there, but also the right to expend any or all of those funds on objects or in ways of their own, not approved by the Parent Society ; thus leaving those who wish to assist the Parent Society no regular and recognized channel for communicating such assistance. This compact, they state, has always been " carefully " observed " from 1839 to 1869 ;" has been repeatedly recognized by the Board of Directors and the Secretary of the Parent Society, and has now been violated. In proof, they quote, not a "compact" between the two Societies, but portions of the Constitution of the American Colonization Society, adopted December 12, 1838, and liable to amendment, as provided in Article XII. :

"There shall be a Board of Directors, composed of Delegates from the several State Societies, and Societies for the District of Columbia, and Territories of the United States."   ·

This, they say, is "in the Fifth Article of the Constitution," "in Section Four ;" but there is no " Section Four " in the "Fifth Article." The words quoted are from Article IV., the whole of which reads thus :

"There shall be a Board of Directors, composed of Delegates from the several State Societies, and Societies for the District of Columbia, and Territories of the United States. Each Society contributing not less than one thousand dollars annually into the common treasury, shall be entitled to two Delegates ; each Society having under its care a colony, shall be entitled to three Delegates ; and every two or more Societies uniting in the support of a colony comprising at least three hundred souls, to three Delegates each. Any individual contributing one thousand dollars to the Society, shall be a Director for life."

By quoting only a part of the Article, they conceal the fact that

14

the greater part of it is now inappropriate and impracticable, and make it appear as if the Board of Directors was composed exclusively of the Delegates from State Societies.

They then quote from the "Fifth Section" words which are in the Fifth Article :

"The Board shall have power to organize and administer a general government, to provide a uniform code of laws for such colonies, and manage the general affairs of colonization throughout the United States, except within the States which planted colonies."

They leave out the words, "for the several colonies in Liberia," after the word "government;" and do not quote, from the conclusion of that Article, the following words :

"It shall be their duty to provide for the fulfillment of all existing obligations of the American Colonization Society ; and nothing in the following Article of these amendments shall limit or restrain their power to make such provision by an equitable assessment upon the several Societies."

They omit wholly the Sixth and Seventh Articles :

"The expenses of the General Government in Africa shall be, borne by the several associated Societies, according to the ratio to be fixed by the Board of Directors."

"Every such Society which has under its care a colony, associated under the General Government, shall have the right to appropriate its own funds in the colonization and care of its emigrants."

It is evident that these constitutional provisions, from which their proof of a "compact," or "pledge," is so skillfully selected, were applicable only to Societies having the care of colonies, bound to meet the expenses of their government, and liable to be assessed by the Board of Directors for the necessary amount. The New York State Colonization Society is not such a Society, nor has it been for twenty-two years past. There has been no State Society to which those provisions could be applied, since the organization of the independent Republic of Liberia, in January, 1848.

Nor is this all. At the meeting of the Directors of the American Colonization Society, in January, 1846, resolutions were passed, advising the people of Liberia to publish a Declaration of

Independence, and to organize a government for themselves ; and the Constitution of the Society was amended to adapt it to the new order of affairs which would be the result. In amending the Constitution, all the clauses on which the New York State Society now relies in proof of a "compact," were stricken out and repealed ; so that they have not been any part of the Constitution, nor in any respect binding on any body, for twenty-four years past.

Such is their proof of " the pledge of non-interference," which the American Colonization Society is accused of violating. It is made up of unfair extracts from constitutional provisions which were never applicable to such a Society as they are and have been for twenty-two years, and which were repealed by the votes of the delegates from New York, as well as others, twenty-four years ago.

And even while the Constitution of 1838 was still in force, these restrictions were found disadvantageous to the general cause, and were relaxed by mutual agreement, as follows :

Extracts from the Minutes of the Board of Directors of the American Colonization, Society, at a meeting held in Washington, D. C., August 18, 1842.

" After mature deliberation, the following resolutions were unanimously adopted, viz.:

" 1. *Resolved,* That the wants of the American Colonization Society imperatively demand more extensive and vigorous efforts in soliciting donations.

"2. *Resolved,* That the present exclusive claim of the respective State Societies, especially in the large and wealthy States, to solicit donations within certain local boundaries, is a serious embarrassment to the efforts of the Parent Society, who are desirous to send agents into such States, and that therefore it is expedient for the Executive Committee of the American Colonization Society to obtain the consent of such Societies for the uncontrolled labor of agents as the best interests of the Parent Society may from time to time require.

"3. *Resolved,* That all State Societies be requested to report and transmit monthly their collections to the Executive Committee of the American Colonization Society, and that if any State Society wishes, the funds collected by the Parent Society shall be credited to the respective State Societies.

" 4. *Resolved,* That the Colony of Liberia needs the continued patronage of the American Colonization Society, and that the great objects, both religious and political, contemplated for Africa and her children, can not be accomplished without more hearty co-operation of the friends of the great and noble cause.

"5. *Resolved*, That the Secretary forward a copy of these resolutions to the various Auxiliary Societies."

"A true copy from the records,

"Wm. Coppinger, *Rec. Sec. A. C. S.*

"Colonization Rooms,
"Washington, D. C., *April* 2, 1870.

"At a meeting of the Board of Managers of the New York State Colonization Society, held within the Colonization Rooms, 142 Nassau Street, New York, on Monday, September 19, 1842, the following resolution was unanimously adopted :

"*Resolved*, That in the present crisis in the cause of colonization, we respond to the proposed efforts by agents within this State, by communicating our full consent, as already given to Mr. Gurley, that the Parent Board shall have our approval of any agencies they may appoint to labor in the State of New York, with the understanding that they are to labor in such places as may be agreed upon in consultation with the Executive Committee of this Board.

"A true copy,
"Alex. Proudfit, *Cor. Sec. N. Y. State Col. Soc.*"

Copy.

"Colonization Rooms,
"Philadelphia, *September* 27, 1842.

"*Gentlemen*:—At a meeting of the Board of Managers of the Pennsylvania Colonization Society, held at this office on the 16th inst., the following resolutions were adopted, viz.:

"*Resolved*, That the resolution of the Board of Directors, passed on the 18th of August, having been submitted and considered, on motion, it was

"*Resolved*, That this Society has ever been anxious to afford every facility and assistance to the American Colonization Society, and do most readily accord to them the permission requested to send their agents into this State, whenever it may promote the common object :

"*Provided*, That if at any time this Society considers this operation evil, this permission may be withdrawn ;

"*And provided further*, That the first moneys collected in this State shall be appropriated to the payment of the two drafts for $675 each, drawn by the late Thomas Buchanan on the New York and Pennsylvania Societies, for goods placed in the Colonial Store at Bassa Cove.

"Extract from the minutes,
"Robert B. Davidson, *Sec. P. T.*"

The Pennsylvania resolutions are none the less authentic because, in the absence of Rev. J. B. Pinney, they were attested by a Secretary *pro tem.*

Neither of those State Societies has yet withdrawn the assent thus given. The resolutions of both remain unrevoked to this day.

THE APPEAL TO PRACTICE.

To strengthen their position as to a "pledge," by an appeal to practice, they affirm :

"And for thirty years from this date, namely, from 1839 to 1869, the American Colonization Society carefully abstained from making any collections in the State of New York."

The proceedings of August and September, 1842, just quoted, show that this was true only in a very modified sense, even from 1839 to 1846, when those restrictions were repealed. The fact is, that during those years collections were made in the State of New York, by at least the following persons, acting as agents of the American Colonization Society, viz. :—In 1839, by Rev. C. Colton; in 1840, by Rev. C. Colton, Rev. R. R. Gurley, Hon. William Halsey, Captain George Barker, and Judge Wilkeson ; in 1841, by Rev. R. R. Gurley and Judge Wilkeson ; in 1842, by Judge Wilkeson, and Rev. J. K. Davis ; in 1843, by Rev. J. K. Davis ; and in 1844, by Rev. S. Cornelius ; and numerous sums were remitted by pastors, collected among their people, and by other friends. In 1846, as we have seen, those restrictive clauses were stricken out of the Constitution, and no regard has been had to them since. Collections were made by Rev. J. K. Davis in 1846 ; by Captain George Barker in 1848 ; by Rev. Wm. McLain, personally, in 1850 ; by Rev. J. M. Pease in 1851 ; by Rev. W. McLain in 1855, and at sundry other times, personally, by letter, and by printed appeals ; and without obtaining or asking permission from the State Society.

In November, 1849, Rev. Wm. McLain appealed through the *African Repository*, for "three thousand dollars, wanted in thirty days," for colonizing sixty slaves who had been left with the privilege of emigrating to Liberia by the will of Thomas Capehart, of Murfreesborough, N. C. The money was received, and acknowledged in the *Repository* for February, 1850. Eleven

2

donations of one hundred dollars each were received from the State of New York, of which eight were from the City.

In April, 1850, he appealed through the New York *Journal of Commerce*, for $1,800 to colonize about thirty, late slaves of Timothy Rodgers, of Bedford County, Va. The Editor, Gerard Hallock, acted as a volunteer agent, gave one hundred dollars himself, procured seventeen other donations of the same amount, and May 10th, paid it over to "J. B. Pinney, Cor. Sec., etc., etc.," who the same day paid it to "Wm. McLain, Sec. and Treas. A. C. S." Among the donors were Anson G. Phelps and Anson G. Phelps, Jr., successive Presidents of the New York State Colonization Society.

In view of these facts, and many others that might be shown, and some of which will be shown, the assertion that "from 1839 to 1869, the American Colonization Society carefully abstained from making any collection in the State of New York," sounds rather strangely. It must have been made without due consideration.

THE ALLEGED RECOGNITION OF THE COMPACT BY THE DIRECTORS.

At the next meeting of the Board of Directors, January 22, 1851, on motion of the Rev. J. B. Pinney, it was

" *Resolved*, That for the purpose of securing entire harmony and co-operation between the State Societies and the Parent Society, all appeals, special or otherwise, for funds, which the Executive Committee may desire to make in any State, should be first communicated to the officers and proper agency of the State Society, and, if possible, made through them."

It is evident, on the face of this resolution, that its mover was not aware of the existence, at that time, of any "compact," "pledge," law, or obligation, restraining the Parent Society from making such appeals anywhere, at its own discretion; nor did he propose to take away its right to make such appeals whenever it should desire, or to authorize the State Societies to take it away in any case; but only to regulate the mode of making them.

The next act but one of the Directors was, to reconsider this resolution, and refer the whole subject to a Committee of five, to report the next morning. That Committee reported a preamble and resolutions, which, after discussion, were adopted, as follows:

"The Committee to whom was referred the resolution offered by Rev. Mr. Pinney, on the subject of appeals made for funds, beg leave to report the following preamble and resolutions, for the consideration of the Board :

" *Whereas* The interests of the colonization cause require that there should be uniformity in its system of operations, and harmony of action and co-operation among the several Societies and agencies engaged in the work ; and *whereas*, it seems necessary, in order to secure this end, that there should be a more full and perfect understanding in regard to the relations between the American Colonization Society and its several auxiliaries, and of the principles upon which their respective operations are to be conducted ; therefore,

"*Resolved*, That all appeals for funds, which the Executive Committee of the Parent Society may desire to make in any State where there is an Auxiliary Society in active operation, should first be communicated to the proper agency of the State Society, and should in all cases be made through them, and that all collections so made should be passed to the credit of said Society on the books of the Executive Committee.

"*Resolved*, That the usefulness and efficiency of the American Colonization Society require the active aid and co-operation of its several auxiliaries ; and in order to this, it is desired and expected that each Auxiliary Society, after defraying its own domestic expenses, will pay over the balance of its funds, if any, to the treasury of the American Society.

"*Resolved*, That in the view of this Board, it is essential to that unity of plan and harmony of action which are requisite in carrying forward successfully the work of colonization, that the several Auxiliary Societies, in their arrangements for sending out emigrants, and in all their business transactions with the Republic of Liberia, should act through, or in co-operation with, the Executive Committee of the Parent Society.

"*Resolved*, further, That in the view of this Board, a compliance with the preceding resolution, in respect to sending out and settling emigrants, is rendered indispensable by the stipulations which exist between the Republic and the American Colonization Society in regard to the occupation of the lands, and in regard to commercial regulations. It is necessary also, in order to secure that uniformity in the provisions made for emigrants, and that disposition of them in the territory, which their own interests and the welfare of the colonists alike demand.

"*Resolved*, That the Executive Committee of the Society be directed to send a copy of the foregoing preamble and resolutions to the several Auxiliary Societies."

Here, also, is no recognition of any " compact," coming down from 1838. There is merely a vote of the Board of Directors, liable to be rescinded at discretion, like any other vote. It applies only to "any State where there is an Auxiliary Society in active operation." And the restriction on the Parent Society in the first resolution is based on the expectation that the auxiliaries will observe the rules laid down for them in the second, third, and fourth.

In August, 1851, the Parent Society found it necessary to issue a special appeal in behalf of the forty-eight "Herndon Slaves," and twenty-three others, of whom eight were free. It was made by circulars addressed to individuals in many States. The money was raised, and the company sent to Liberia. At the meeting of the Directors in January, 1855, so much of the Annual Report as related to this matter was referred to a Special Committee, on whose recommendation the following preamble and resolution were adopted, viz. :

"The Committee to whom was referred that portion of the Annual Report which relates to special appeals from the Corresponding Secretary for funds to meet particular cases, with instructions to consider and report upon the best mode of preventing the conflict between such appeals and the regular work of the agents of the State Societies, beg leave to report :

"That they have considered the subject committed to them, and are of the opinion that it is necessary to the best interests of the work which we have in hand, and to the prudence, wisdom, and economy of time, effort, and money, by which all our operations ought to be characterized, that as far as practicable all possibility of interference between the plans and acts of the Central Board at Washington and those of any of the State Societies should be prevented. Such interference—unintentional, your Committee are persuaded—has occurred during the past year in more than one instance, and been productive of harm and loss, notwithstanding the resolution of the Board of Directors passed at the annual meeting in 1851.

"With the view of preventing the occurrence of similar evils, your Committee recommend the adoption of the following resolution :

"Resolved, That hereafter all appeals from the Corresponding Secretary, the General Agent, or the Executive Committee, for funds for any purpose connected with the objects of the American Colonization Society in States wherein Auxiliary Societies exist, shall be made only through said Societies, and under their direction."

This, it will be perceived, makes no change, except in holding the Parent Society more strictly to the modes of appeal directed by the State Societies. It assumes that the appeals will still continue to be made, and that the State Societies will do their duty in directing the mode of making them. It gives no State Society any power to exclude such appeals wholly, and turn all the benefactions of the friends of colonization into its own treasury, to be expended on its own projects, whether the donors wish it or not.

It leaves the obligation of every auxiliary to pay over the balance of its funds, after defraying its domestic expenses, to the Parent Society, and to act only through or in co-operation with the Executive Committee of the Parent Society, in full force.

The resolution first passed in 1851, restricting the Parent Society unconditionally, was reconsidered and rejected, and in its stead a series of resolutions was adopted, restricting it only on certain conditions to be observed by the State Societies.

These conditions, established by the resolutions of 1851 and left unimpaired by that of 1855, the New York State Colonization Society has habitually disregarded. Instead of paying over " the balance of its funds," after defraying its own domestic expenses, " to the treasury of the American Society," or in sending out emigrants " through, or in co-operation with, the Executive Committee of the Parent Society," it has expended a part of them in sending out emigrants independently of the Parent Society, and often without consulting the Executive Committee, and by conveyances and at rates of expense which that Committee would not have recommended. But a larger portion of that "balance" was expended for many years in projects so distinct from the operations of the Parent Society, that no such claim was advanced in respect to it. As this last sentence is based on a statement made by one of the Delegates from that State Society, in a carefully prepared speech before the Board of Directors at their last annual meeting, its correctness will not probably be questioned.

One instance of this kind deserves special mention ; that of the Seth Grosvenor, a steamer of seventy tons, built and sent out for service on the African coast. Their vote authorizing it, June 10, 1859, appropriated only ten thousand dollars for that purpose ; but their Report for 1861 says, that " in the progress of completing the vessel and sending her across the ocean, the sum originally contemplated was doubled." This was done not only without the co-operation of the Parent Society, but against its earnest remonstrance. The enterprise proved a failure, as had been foreseen. The steamer was sold at Sierra Leone, and their Report for 1864 acknowledges the receipt of $4,375 as its net proceeds. Whether that sum, or any part of it, was ever remitted to New York, or whether the whole had been absorbed by expenses on the coast, we are not informed. During the years of this operation, and, it is understood, as a means of executing it, that Society, in its capacity as a Society, borrowed of itself in its capacity as a Trustee of Funds for Education, about twenty thousand dollars, as appears from its Annual Reports. This loan was paid by installments from year to year, from the general funds of the Society, given for the purposes of colonization, which ought, according to the resolutions of 1851, to have been paid over to the treasury of the Parent Society.

THE RESOLUTIONS OF THE DIRECTORS HAVE BEEN OBEYED.

With such a record, the New York State Society has no right to claim a strict observance of the restrictive resolutions of 1851 and 1855. And yet the Executive Committee at Washington did not disregard them. The "Synopsis" itself expressly asserts that they were "carefully" observed up to the year 1869. It appears from the "Synopsis," and more fully from the State Society's "Statement," that in August, 1866, the Financial Secretary at Washington asked of the State Society, "permission to make an appeal for aid" in that State ; referring, not to any ancient "compact," but to the resolution of 1855, as his reason for not doing it, as in the case of the Herndon slaves, without their consent ; that the State Society, in September, 1866, gave its assent "to the American Society, sending a Collecting Agent" into that State ; that accordingly, in 1866, the Rev. Dr. Orcutt, Traveling Secretary, made some collections in that State ; that early in 1867 "he came to New York and commenced a Collecting Agency" there ; that the State Society received him with cordiality and aided him in his work ; that even after the remarkable "annual election" in May, 1868, "a resolution was passed by the Board of Managers, permitting the continuance of the agency of the Traveling Secretary in the State," and that "this permission continued until February, 1869." It also appears, as it were involuntarily and unconsciously, that this permission has never been withdrawn to this day. An attempt was made to withdraw it, May 23, 1868, when, as the "Synopsis" states, the following resolution was offered :

"Resolved, That, inasmuch as this Society is now prepared to recommence its work in the State of New York, the resolution passed September 10, 1866, authorizing the American Colonization Society to make collections in this State, be rescinded from and after the close of this month ; and that a copy of this resolution be communicated to the said Society."

If the State Society had then possessed the right which it erroneously claims, of excluding the Parent Society wholly from the State, this resolution was in the proper form for exercising that right. By it, the State Society took upon itself the whole responsibility of Dr. Orcutt's removal. It left nothing for him or the Parent Society to do, but to submit.

But this resolution was not passed. It was deferred till after the annual election, which was to occur May 30th. After that election, as we have already seen from the "Statement," the Managers took up the question which had been deferred, and instead of adopting the resolution offered May 23d, passed a resolution "permitting the continuance " of Dr. Orcutt's labors there.

These proceedings, and some others, show the existence, at that time, of two parties, more or less distinctly formed, in the State Society ; one desiring Dr. Orcutt's continuance, and the other his removal. The latter was not able to carry its point in the Board of Managers, till February, 1869 ; and even then they did not carry a vote passing the resolution offered May 23, 1868, assuming the responsibility of Dr Orcutt's removal, but instead of it, passed a vote "respectfully requesting " the Parent Society to assume it. The vote was in the following words :

" *Resolved*, That the American Colonization Society at Washington be, and is hereby, respectfully requested, by the New York State Colonization Society, to transfer Rev. Dr. Orcutt, now laboring in New York, to another field of labor."

What induced this change of phraseology ; whether they had some misgivings as to their right to order him out of the State ; whether they could not get a majority of the Managers present to pass such a vote ; or whether it was mere courtesy, we are not informed. If courtesy, it was a courtesy which changed the very nature of their act, by placing the responsibility for his removal on other shoulders than their own. Their " permission," therefore is not yet " rescinded."

DR. ORCUTT'S CONTINUANCE AT NEW YORK.

For several reasons, the Parent Society did not assume that responsibility. One was, the following protest, signed by eight members of their Board of Managers,—one more than a quorum :

"The undersigned respectfully dissent from the resolution, adopted February 23, 1869, by this Board, requesting the American

Colonization Society to transfer their Secretary, Rev. Dr. Orcutt, to some other field of labor, because

" 1. There is no other agency to promote the objects of the American Colonization Society in this State, except that which was established here by the resolution under which Dr. Orcutt came to this field.

" 2. The Secretary of the New York State Colonization Society is not friendly to the operations of the American or Parent Society, and his public statements are calculated to prevent, rather than to secure, contributions for its support.

" 3. As a large number of the friends of the cause residing in this State prefer to contribute through the Parent Society, it was agreed in June last to renew the invitation to the Parent Society to continue its agency here, and the withdrawal of that invitation now, without a conference, is a breach of faith, and an act of discourtesy.

" 4. The election of officers at the last annual meeting was carried by the sudden manufacture of voters previously unknown and having no interest whatever in the Society or the cause ; and in the resolution from which we dissent, we find a determination to carry out a policy destructive to the harmony of the Society, and subversive of confidence among those who are acting together in the furtherance of a great and philanthropic work.

" 5. The Government of Liberia being firmly established, and having sufficient intelligence to manage its internal affairs, and the several Missionary Boards of the Presbyterian, Episcopal, and Methodist churches being actively engaged in the advancement of education in Liberia, it may be safely left to the government and the churches, with such aid as our vested funds and voluntary contributions to the cause may afford.

" 6. The trust funds held by this Society should be faithfully applied to the specific purpose for which they were given, and not to general purposes unmentioned in the deeds of gift ; the integrity of the Trustees being pledged to such fidelity, and the safety of the property itself requiring the utmost caution in this respect ; and the undersigned regarding the recent appropriation of money from the Bloomfield fund to the purchase of books, etc., for schools, as not consistent with the objects of the bequest (which appropriation has since been charged to general fund), and regarding the resolution of last week as indicating a determination to carry out a line of policy not in harmony with the original spirit and purposes of this Society, are constrained respectfully to express their dissent from these proceedings, and to enter their dissent upon the minutes, with permission of the Board.

" They further request that a copy of this dissent may be trans-

mitted to the Parent Society with a copy of the resolution passed
February 23, 1869.

"S. Irenæus Prime.	"Thomas De Witt.
"Benjamin I. Haight.	"H. K. Bull.
"Moses Allen.	"A. Merwin.
"John N. McLeod.	"D. S. Gregory."

The resolution against which these eight Managers protest
may have been passed by a vote of four to three, when a bare
quorum was present.*

THE DIVISION IN THE NEW YORK STATE SOCIETY.

In order to understand all the bearings of this resolution and
protest, it is necessary briefly to sketch another series of acts,
running back several years.

Early in the late civil war, Rev. Dr. Pinney attempted to procure emigrants to Liberia among the "contrabands," as they were
then called. In January, 1863, he and "James Mitchell, Com-
missioner of Emigration for the United States," presented a "memorial" to the United States Senate, praying for an appropriation
"to aid and encourage the emigration of all classes of our free
colored population." The Secretary of War would not permit
him to go among the contrabands, to ascertain their willingness
to emigrate. On the failure of this plan, the New York State Society, as appears from its own "Statement," "resolved to suspend
its agencies, and reduce its expenses to the smallest sum consistent with the maintenance of its organization and the administra-
tion of the trust funds, which had been given to it for educational
purposes." Dr. Pinney tendered his resignation as Corresponding Secretary ; but instead of its acceptance, he received leave of
absence, and remained in nominal connection with the Society,
but "for the greater part of the time without salary." He engaged, first, in growing cotton near the Mississippi River, and
afterward in mining for silver in Nevada. The Society's office
was left in charge of Mr. J. M. Goldberg, who conducted its cor-
respondence as its "Secretary." The "Synopsis" calls him "an.

---

* It is said that eight were present, and that the vote was five to three.

assistant to the Secretary." For a part of the time, another organization or two occupied its office, with or without paying rent.

Such was the state of affairs when Dr. Orcutt commenced his labors in New York, as above narrated ; with the additional fact, that some of its most valuable members and officers had abstained from taking any part in its proceedings for several years. For all purposes, except the custody of the trust funds, the Society had been virtually disorganized. An attempt was made by most of its active members, and many who had long been inactive, to reorganize it and restore its efficiency. At a meeting of a quorum of the Managers, March 3, 1868, G. P. Disosway, Esq., an old and every way reliable friend of the cause, and a member of the Board of Managers, was chosen Secretary, and immediately entered on the duties of that office. Six Managers, March 5th, protested against this election, as made at a meeting not regularly called. At the next regular meeting, March 17th, " it was stated that Rev. Dr. Pinney was shortly expected to return." He had previously informed Dr. Orcutt, that he should never return to resume his former place and labors, and it was so understood by others. At this meeting, Mr. Disosway was formally chosen Secretary. Of course, he could hold the office only till the next annual election. At the next meeting, May 23d, a paper was presented, concluding : " It is also our earnest wish that Hon. G. P. Disosway be retained as Secretary of the State Society, to co-operate with the Parent Society's agency in its efforts for the further promotion of the great and good cause." This, as printed in the " Synopsis," was signed by six officers of the Society, and thirteen others, doubtless members. Of the six officers, it is said that four had not attended a meeting of the Board for nine years or more. It seems that they had not lost their interest in the cause, nor in the Society if, managed as it was then, and as they hoped that it would continue to be. The copy before us contains the names of eight officers and twenty-nine others ; some having been added, probably, between May 23d and May 30th, the day of the annual election. This paper, it will be seen, was well adapted to alarm any who might wish to displace Mr. Disosway, and to change the policy of the Society. After reading it, the following resolution, before quoted, was offered, but not passed :

" *Resolved,* That, inasmuch as this Society is now prepared to recommence its work in the State of New York, the resolution passed September 10, 1866, authorizing the American Colonization Society to make collections in this State, be rescinded from and after the close of the present month ; and that a copy of this resolution be communicated to the said Society."

This resolution plainly admits that the Society had been in a condition in which it was not "prepared" to carry on "its work," and discloses the desire of its mover to change the policy of the Society from that requested in the paper which had just been read, to something else.

THE ELECTION IN 1868.

At the annual election, May 30th, the action of those desiring a change was most extraordinary. There have been some faint and feeble attempts at palliation, but nobody defends it, and the Society disclaims responsibility for it. According to the "Statement," there were present " twenty-eight persons who had recently become members, some of them by the contribution of one" of the Board of Managers, whose "avowed object was" to control the election by their votes. " Whether the act was or was not wise, it was his act, and not the act of the Society or its Board of Managers." The "Synopsis" says : "For their presence the New York State Society or its Board of Managers are in no way responsible." Yet somebody was certainly responsible for the receiving and counting of their votes, in violation both of the words and the intent of the Constitution of that Society. The Constitutions of some Societies provide that the contribution of a specified sum shall constitute the donor a member " for one year from the time of such donation." That of the New York State Society was more safely drawn. As it was then, it read :

" ART. 3. The subscription or donation of not less than one dollar annually shall constitute an individual a member of this Society ; and the payment, at one time, of thirty dollars, a membership for life."

There must be either a subscription, a written promise to pay one dollar "annually," or a practice of paying one dollar "annually," indicating some permanent interest in the Society, to constitute one a member. The Constitution did not add :

" And any person desirous to control an election may create the requisite number of new members, pledged to vote as he wishes, by paying that number of dollars to an assistant of the Secretary."

Such was neither its language nor its intent; and therefore an election controlled in that way was unconstitutional, null and void in law, and conferred on those so elected no right to perform any official duty.

The presiding Vice-President, after some unsatisfactory attempts to enforce the rules of order among these "new members" and those who had brought them in, left the chair and the room, and was followed by at least five other officers of the Society. Those who remained, elected Rev. J. B. Pinney, LL.D., Corresponding Secretary, and J. M. Goldberg Recording Secretary. Mr. Disosway was allowed to retain his place on the Board of Managers, but was otherwise unnoticed.

The six officers who withdrew, that very evening signed a call for a meeting "of old and tried friends of the colonization cause, to consider and determine what steps it may be necessary to take in this crisis of the affairs of the Society." That meeting, holden June 3d, denounced the election by members thus made, as not only at variance with propriety and honor, "but also a flagrant violation of the true intent and spirit of the Constitution of the Society, and therefore utterly illegal and void." It was also resolved that a Provisional Committee be appointed, "to take such steps as the welfare of the Society and interests of African Colonization may appear to them to demand;" that the arrangement for the collection of funds by Dr. Orcutt and Mr. Disosway should be continued till the next annual meeting; and that another meeting be holden June 8th, for organizing the Committee. At that meeting a Provisional Committee was appointed of ten members, of whom seven were members of the Board of Directors of the New York State Society, and Mr. Disosway, another Director, was appointed its Secretary.

Yet those who had controlled the election by introducing "new members," were not able at once to govern the Society. At the first meeting of the Board of Directors, the resolution for excluding the Parent Society from the State, which had been put over from May 23d, could not be passed; but instead of it, a resolution was passed, continuing the collection of funds by Dr. Orcutt and Mr. Disosway, "during the current year," that is, till the annual meeting in May, 1869. Dr. Orcutt's continuance, therefore, had the sanction both of the Directors elected May 30th, and of the

Provisional Committee of those who pronounced that election "illegal and void." It was not till February, 1869, near the close of that "current year," that a majority of a quorum of those whose right to their offices was thus in dispute, voted—not to pass the resolution offered May 23, 1868, rescinding Dr. Orcutt's permission to labor in the State, but to request the Parent Society to transfer him to another field of labor. The Provisional Committee, containing Directors enough to form a quorum, still desired his continuance. There had been no legal decision of the question, whether they were not the true and lawful conservators of the Society. In these circumstances, the Parent Society did not assume the responsibility of transferring Dr. Orcutt.

THE REVOLUTION COMPLETED.

At the annual meeting in May, 1869, the "new men," by whom the election in 1868 had been controlled, completed their revolution in the State Society. They amended their Constitution so as to make it impossible that any future election should be controlled as that of the previous year had been. They reduced the number of officers to twenty-four, thus getting rid of many "old, long tried" friends of the Parent Society. They appointed eight "new men" as members of the Board of Managers, and provided that seven should be a quorum.

This new Constitution was adopted May 28, 1869. The same day, the Board of Managers passed a resolution adopting their new policy, founded on their new discovery, that the Parent Society could not promote education in Liberia. In June, the war of circulars and pamphlets against the Parent Society commenced.

THE NEW YORK COLONIZATION SOCIETY.

Dr. Orcutt continued to labor in connection with the Provisional Committee, till those whose views that Committee represented formed their new organization, the New York Colonization Society, making it strictly auxiliary to the American Colonization Society. Since then, he has been laboring in connection with that Society by its express invitation.

CONCLUSION.

The "Memorial" of the State Society requests, in its last paragraph, that this arrangement be broken up. It requests the

American Colonization Society, "in pursuance of the compact between the two Societies, to withdraw all agencies from the State of New York, and leave its territory to be canvassed by the New York State Society's agents." And such must be the aim of this "Statement" and "Synopsis," if they aim at anything but creating a prejudice against the Parent Society and its new auxiliary. It has been shown that no such "compact" exists; that what they erroneously claim as such a "compact" was repealed twenty-four years ago, and has never been recognized since; that citizens of New York who disapprove of the course of the State Society, and wish to sustain the American, have a right to form an Auxiliary Society for that purpose, and to be recognized and represented as an auxiliary, and to receive from the Parent Society the same aid and encouragement as any other auxiliary. The "request," therefore, can not be granted, and the State Society has no right to complain that it is not granted.

THEIR APPENDIX.

The Appendix to the "Statement" contains a few extracts from anonymous letters, disparaging the operations of the Parent Society. They are such as somebody can be induced to write anonymously at any time, about any enterprise, and are disproved by authentic information, received at the office of the Parent Society from well-known and reliable witnesses, much of which is published from time to time in the *African Repository*. They need no other answer.

HARVEY LINDSLY, *Chairman,*
JOSEPH H. BRADLEY,
WILLIAM GUNSTON,
GEORGE W. SAMSON,
PETER PARKER,
SAMUEL H. HUNTINGTON,
JOHN B. KERR,

} *Executive Committee of the American Colonization Society.*

WILLIAM McLAIN, *Financial Secretary, Am. Col. Soc.*
WILLIAM COPPINGER, *Cor. and Rec. Sec. " " "*

COLONIZATION ROOMS,
WASHINGTON, D. C., *May* 6, 1870.

LETTERS

FROM THE

TRAVELING SECRETARY

AND

REV. DR. MACLEAN,

LATE PRESIDENT OF PRINCETON COLLEGE.

---

24 Bible House, New York City, *May* 17, 1870.

To the Ex-Committee of the Am. Col. Soc.

Gentlemen :—I have read your "Exposition," etc., and desire to say that there are certain allegations made against me personally in the documents therein reviewed, which seem to demand of me some further notice.

In regard to the charge of falsehood contained in what professes to be an extract from my letter of February 3, 1869, and is quoted on page 9 of the "Statement," nothing, perhaps, need be added. But as the quotation is a material *perversion* of my language, it is proper that I should state just what I did say, which was this : "The amount the Parent Society has received in *cash* from the New York State Colonization Society *since* 1849—nearly twenty years—is less than $12,000 ; and the entire amount *claimed by the State Society as a basis of representation*, has not averaged $1,000 a year for the last fifteen years, or more ;" and this saying you have clearly shown to be according to the facts in the case.

On page 11 of the "Statement," I am charged with "intruding myself into a Committee duly appointed to nominate officers, with a view to prevent the nomination and re-election of the Corresponding Secretary ; and subsequently of obtruding myself into the meeting held for the election, not being an elector."

I have no knowledge of ever being present at a meeting of the New York State Colonization Society, or of its Committee, convened for the nomination of officers. By special request of prominent members and officers of the Society, I did attend the annual meeting referred to, but remained only till the chairman and other influential members left the room on account of what soon occurred.

On page 23 of the same document, I am charged with disregarding a resolution of the State Society, granting permission to the Parent Society to make collections in the State, in not "paying them through the Treasurer of our Society."

It is true that none of the money I have collected in New York has taken that course ; and the simple reason is, that said "Treasurer" *persistently* refused to take it ; saying he did not want the trouble of it, and that it would be just as well for me to make the remittances and report the amount to him. Accordingly I did so, until the appointment of the "Provisional Committee," who instructed me to make my reports to them. Besides, during my labors in the State, my collections have been acknowledged in the *African Repository* every month, to the credit of New York.

Other charges and insinuations preferred against me I will forbear to notice, except to say, they are all as groundless as those I have specified.

I commenced my labors in this State, with no other purpose or desire than, to awaken a new interest in the cause to which I had devoted nearly twenty years of my life ; and in all my efforts in this behalf here, as in other States, I have aimed to secure *harmony* and *efficiency* among our friends in prosecuting the work in hand.

Very respectfully yours,

JOHN ORCUTT.

PRINCETON, April 5, 1870.

My Dear Sir :—I see, by a pamphlet recently issued by the Board of the New York State Colonization Society, that they have determined to continue their attacks upon the American Colonization Society, and to do us all the harm they can, simply, as I conceive the matter, for the reason that we will not yield to their unreasonable demands. Whether it is best to take any notice of this last effusion, I have my doubts. Not because there would be any difficulty in answering their statements, and showing the unreasonableness of their conduct ; but for the reason that probably we might employ our time better in direct efforts to interest the Christian community in the efforts of the American Society, to promote the welfare of the colored race. We have a definite and a most important work to do. We must, by the use of every legitimate means in our power, add to the numbers and to the efficiency of the Liberian Republic, and do all we can to make Liberia attractive to the emigrants from this country. Should we succeed in this, the reflex action upon the colored people in the United States can not fail to be most happy, whether they go or stay.

If it should be found to be the case, that these assaults are seriously interfering with our work, and that they have alienated from us the kind feelings of any considerable number of our Christian friends, then we must devote some of our time to replying to their charges and statements. And in this case, I will endeavor to do my part in the matter, as I fully approve the course of the American Colonization Society, and at the last meeting of the Directors, advocated even more stringent measures than those adopted by the Board of Directors. But after the compromise made by the Board, by admitting the Delegates from both the New York Societies, in which all parties acquiesced (if they did not all vote), I made no further attempt to urge my own views, or even to reply to some remarks to which I certainly should have replied, had I not thought that the adoption of the compromise required me to waive all further discussion. I certainly was surprised that the pamphlet referred to at the beginning of this letter should have made any mention of the memorial from the " Board of Control," of the New York State Colonization Society, which our Board, after hearing it read, I might perhaps say a second time, and the first time with copious comments by its author, laid upon the table by the decisive vote of 15 to 5, the first vote for laying it on the table being that of the honored President of the New York State Society. These facts it did not suit the writer of the pamphlet to mention. It would have exposed the unreasonableness, not to say absurdity, of his complaints, to have done so.

With sincere esteem, yours, etc.,

Rev. Dr. Orcutt.   John Maclean.

3

STATEMENT

OF THE

NEW YORK COLONIZATION SOCIETY.

THE Executive Committee of this Society, in view of certain pamphlets which have recently appeared from the office of the New York State Colonization Society, deem it expedient to offer to their constituents and friends the following observations :

I.—It seems hardly necessary to say in this community, where the founders and officers of our Society are so well known, and have been for many years, that the Society was not created by any other Association, or by any of its Agents, acting either directly or indirectly. To affirm this is simply ridiculous. The statement of such an absurdity is its own abundant refutation.

II.—Neither is it the fact that our Society was founded in ill will and antagonism to any person or persons, or with any design to interfere with the due official prerogatives and proper influence of any existing functionary. That any such low and unworthy motives actuated the men who founded our Society is another palpable absurdity and baseless insinuation.

III.—Our Society was formed simply because of the conviction forced upon the minds of a number of the old friends of African Colonization, and supporters of the American Colonization Society, that the dominant influence in the State Colonization Society was not in harmony with the Parent Institution, and that for the due support of that Institution by means of direct contributions to its Treasury, and by co-operation in the Board of Directors, a new organization was imperatively demanded. This conviction was of slow growth, but at length it became so deep and potent that it could no longer be resisted. Subsequent events and especially certain proceedings at the late annual meeting of the Parent Institution, and afterward, have shown, unmistakably, the truth of that conviction, and proved that our Society was not prematurely or unwisely formed. That the leading members of the State Colonization Society who controlled the actions of its Managers are sincere in the views which they entertain as to the proper course to be followed in the work of African Colonization, we are far from denying. But those views are not the views of a large number of the friends of that work in New York and elsewhere, and have not been and are not the views of the Directors of the American Colonization Society. They are not the views of those who formed and those who have joined our Association. The difference is one of principles and measures. And it is a serious difference, and one that admits not of compromise. And yet, so far as our Society is concerned, it is a difference which has led to no hard feeling, to no bitter words, and to no invidious allegations in regard to those from whom we dissent. Difference of views in regard to principles and measures in a great philanthropic movement need not and ought not to lead to acrimonious disputation, or to personal crimination and recrimination. And that it shall not produce these wretched results, so far as we are concerned, has been and is our solemn determination.

IV.—Never in the history of African Colonization has there been a greater call for vigorous effort and liberal contributions than at the present. Never was the future so full of promise. Never have the grand philanthropic objects and aims of the American Colonization Society been more clearly perceived and truly appreciated than by many leading men of this generation. This, then, is the time for wise and thoughtful counsel—for prudent and energetic and combined action. The welfare of thousands of the Africans in this country—the welfare of that Christian republic which has been planted on the shores of Africa, and the welfare of the millions now living in darkness and degradation in that benighted continent, alike now demands at the hands of American philanthropists, of American Christians, that they should redouble their interest in the work of the American Colonization Society, and greatly augment their contributions to its treasury. This is the time to send out all proper applicants for a home in Liberia. This is the time to confer fully, and freely. and frankly with the more enlightened of the people of color around us, and to furnish them with reliable information touching the condition and prospects of Liberia. This is the time to strengthen that republic by the expression of our cordial sympathy, and by lending a helping hand to the furtherance of all proper efforts in behalf of the Christian education of its citizens, and especially of the youth.

We give utterance to these thoughts in the hope that they may find a lodgment in many hearts, remove all misapprehensions as to the origin, purpose, and efforts of our Society, and lead, by God's blessing, to an increased interest in the work to which we are pledged, and to constant and liberal gifts to that noble Institution (of which we are an auxiliary), which has now for more than half a century labored faithfully and successfully in behalf of the regeneration of Africa.

BENJ. I. HAIGHT,
S. D. ALEXANDER,
H. K. BULL,
A. MERWIN,
J. D. VERMILYE,
H. G. MARQUAND,

Ex. Com. of N. Y.
Col. Soc.

No. 24 Bible House, New York,
    May 16, 1870

Contributions may be sent to A. Merwin, Esq., Treasurer ; or to Rev. John Orcutt, D. D., one of the Secretaries of the Parent Society, of whose valuable assistance the Executive Committee are happy to avail themselves, having entire confidence in his ability, integrity, and faithful devotion to the cause in which he labors.

Address : Room 24, Bible House, Astor Place, New York.

www.ingramcontent.com/pod-product-compliance
Lightning Source LLC
Chambersburg PA
CBHW021449090426
42739CB00009B/1695